LOOK OUT! HERE COMES THE STANLEY STEAMER

by K. C. *TESSENDORF* illustrated by GLORIA *KAMEN*

Atheneum   1984   New York

Look Out!
Here Comes
The Stanley Steamer

The author and illustrator would like to thank Paul, Don, and Curtis Bourdon, Stanley Steamer collectors, and Mr. Frank Hale Gardner, former president of the Museum of Transportation, Brookline, Massachusetts, for their helpful suggestions and information about the Stanleys and their Steamers.

Library of Congress Cataloging in Publication Data

Tessendorf, K. C.
Look out! here comes the Stanley Steamer.

Summary: Discusses the development of the Stanley Steamer automobile by identical twins F. E. and F. O. Stanley.
1. Stanley Steamer automobile—Juvenile literature.   2. Stanley, Francis Edgar, 1849-1918—Juvenile literature.   3. Stanley, Freelan Oscar, 1849-1940—Juvenile literature.   [1. Stanley Steamer automobile. 2. Automobiles, Steam.   3. Stanley, Francis Edgar, 1849-1918. 4. Stanley, Freelan Oscar, 1849-1940]   I. Kamen, Gloria ill.   II. Title.
TL200.T47   1984   629.2'222   83-15661
ISBN 0-689-31028-5

Published simultaneously in Canada by
McClelland & Stewart, Ltd.
Composition by Dix Type Inc., Syracuse, New York
Printed and bound by The Halliday Lithograph Corporation,
West Hanover, Massachusetts
Typography by Mary Ahern
First Edition

Contents

LOOK OUT!
HERE COMES
THE STANLEY
STEAMER

Legendary Fame

One thousand dollars! That's what they said the Stanley twins would pay the fool driver who dared to pull the throttle wide open on one of their steam automobiles and hold it there for three whole minutes. They would pay him *if* he lived to collect the money.

That was the story being told among young dudes hanging out at American garages in the early twentieth century when the automobile was a new invention and anything seemed possible for it. This story was not true, but it could have been. The last man who tried to hold the throttle wide open had to give up at the two-minute mark when his Stanley Steamer started to take off into the wild blue yonder!

Well, anything could happen with a Stanley Steamer—people really believed that. It was the most wonderful early American automobile built. Of course automobiles like this don't just happen. In this case, there were twin geniuses and a remarkable story behind the building and bringing to fame of the Stanley Steamer.

1.
Down East on the Farm

It was back in 1849 that the Stanley twins, Francis E. and Freelan O., were born. No one besides their family paid much attention to their arrival. Stanleys were so common in the southern part of the State of Maine that it was said a green apple tossed into the air would certainly hit a Stanley.

That was a long time ago. Try to imagine an America without electricity, automobiles, or even running water piped into houses. Cities were small and few because there were not many factories or offices. Americans worked at home, fed and clothed themselves without going to a supermarket or a department store. People didn't have to use much cash money. They were able to grow, make, or harvest from nature nearly everything they needed at home. Americans in 1849 were strong individuals in sturdy family groups working and helping together.

Most of the people, including the Solomon Stanley family, were then farmers. Life down on the farm was simple compared with our times. For example, no tractors, mechanical harvesters, or milking machines were on hand. But the American farm of 1849 had its "labor-saving appliances." They were the children, who were both loved and useful, and there were likely at least half a dozen of them around to help out. On the Stanley farm there were seven children.

Around the house they pumped water, chopped wood, worked the butter churn, made beds, sewed and spun clothing, beat rugs, rubbed laundry on a washboard, cooked food, canned vegetables, washed dishes, looked after younger sisters and brothers.

In the fields they plowed the soil, planted seeds, cultivated and weeded the crops, milked the cows, sheared sheep, fed the poultry. There were special school holidays like October's "Potato Vacation" when it was time to go into the fields and dig up the spuds. Yes, children were VIP workers down on the farm in 1849.

So what would you think happened to these kids when they grew up skilled to be farmers on their own? Well, there was only one home place, only one of the family would stay there. The rest had to move on, some out to the new states in the Middle West, Illinois, Wisconsin, Iowa, where there was vacant fertile ground.

Boys who thought that farming was dull might become lumberjacks in the northern forests, or if adventurous, go off to dig for gold in California. Girls could get household jobs in Boston or New York City, or in the shoe and clothing mills that were being built in southern New England.

But none of these vocations came to Francis E. and Freelan O. Stanley. They were different right from the start, identical twins with shared personalities and skills and they were very close; they knew each other very well. They worked as hard as anyone at farm tasks but they added something extra. They were native geniuses in mechanical know-how. Acting together, they could figure out how to make things work better around the house and barn. Having practical inventors around the place was great!

For one thing, they were skilled whittlers, an important talent in the do-it-yourself times of the last century before ours. A penknife carving odd

pieces of wood could fashion an amazing range of thingamajigs. The United States Patent Office of that era was kept busy considering the inventions of inspired whittlers.

Father Solomon saw early on that the twins were very bright boys. Beside being a farmer, Mr. Stanley was the part-time schoolmaster of their farm community. He counseled his boys to follow him into teaching careers. They took their father's advice and studied long enough to become full-time school teachers. Thereby, they were able to stay near home, working in a professional job. Both young men married girls of the neighborhood and settled down, saving as they could.

2.
Twin Geniuses in the Factory & on the Road

By the late 1870s, America was ready for the Industrial Revolution. Opportunities for inventive geniuses were never greater! F.E. and F.O., as they thought of themselves, were in tune with the times and sure of their natural talent for mechanics. They were on the lookout for a business opportunity. Though identical twins, F.E. was the stronger, bolder personality of the brothers. He had discovered he had an artistic talent and began drawing portraits of friends and neighbors. It was natural that his interest would continue into photography, an expanding marvel of the times, so that he became an expert portrait photographer. When F.E. heard of a photographer's shop in Lewiston, Maine, that was about to go into bankruptcy he talked with his brother about buying it. F.O. agreed that he should take the chance. He was sure F.E. would succeed. And when the time comes that you need me there, I'll come too, F.O. told his twin brother.

So F.E. used his savings of five hundred dollars (about the value of two thousand dollars today) to buy up the failing business. At that time a rival photographer in the town declared that young F.E. would lose his shirt—he wouldn't last six months. But after a year F.E. had not only succeeded in making good in his own business, he also bought out his rival's business and made him his employee! Soon he was making money at three locations. Money-making is one thing, genius another. F.E. now invented an important technical breakthrough in photography, and F.O. joined him in Lewiston.

Early photography was a drippy mess. The chemical solution able to capture the exposure image was applied wet to the glass plate which "took" the picture. It was wasteful, haphazard and time-consuming. It was in 1883 that F.E. figured out how to apply the proper chemicals to the plate in a dry form beforehand. F.E. and F.O. then went ahead and invented the shop machinery to manufacture the new process.

The making of the dry-chemical plates, dryplating, became such a business success that the brothers needed a factory. They sold their Lewiston business and moved down to Newton, Massachusetts, near Boston, where rail connections were better, and opened a plant to manufacture their invention in large quantity. It was the right move and the Stanleys prospered as photographic manufacturers.

In 1896, the twins' engineering interest was drawn to a new marvel of the machine age—the automobile. By the late 1890s, there were several hundred in the United States of America. Most of them were steam-driven.

The nineteenth century was the heyday of the steam engine. Factory machinery turned by the pressure of steam; steamboats were the masters of rivers and oceans. And the railroads of that day could not have operated without steam locomotives. The steam locomotive was the model for the steam automobiles, just appearing on the streets of America.

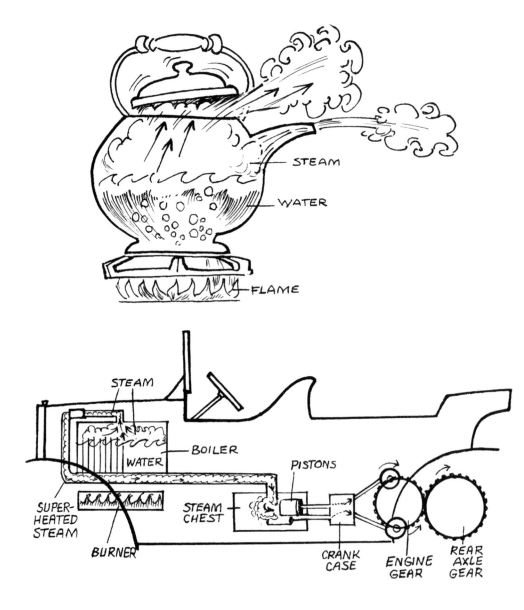

STEAM

WATER

FLAME

STEAM

BOILER

WATER

SUPER-
HEATED
STEAM

BURNER

STEAM
CHEST

PISTONS

CRANK
CASE

ENGINE
GEAR

REAR
AXLE
GEAR

The Stanleys looked over the four-wheeled contraptions then puttering and sputtering around the Boston area and did not care for what they saw. The autos' weakness, their habit of breaking down every mile or two challenged the mechanical genius of the twins. F.E. and F.O. agreed they could do better themselves.

The first decision the brothers had to make was about the type of engine they would use to drive the wheels of their automobile. This engine could be powered by steam, gasoline, or electricity. F.E. and F.O. set aside electricity because a battery-powered automobile of that time would have little power. The potential pep of steam or gasoline engines was more attractive.

The pressure that can be put to work when water is heated into steam is readily seen in the actions of a tea kettle lid and spout. A boiler is a large-scale tea kettle put to work within a steam engine. Controlled steam pressure from the boiler pushes against a piston, moving within the cylinder. The piston passes its force along a series of rods, shafts, gears into the rear wheels, driving them forward or backward.

That is how a steam engine drove a steam automobile.

Early steam engines needed at least two cylinders working together. The rod attached to the bottom of one piston within its cylinder was coupled to a shaft that attached to the rod from the other piston. This forced one piston up into its cylinder while the other was being pushed down by the steam pressure as long as there was controlled steam pressure available from the boiler.

Properly adjusted, it produced a smooth, steady, quiet type of automotive power. Of course, it took some time to heat up water, by a kerosene-fired ring, until it became steam within the boiler. "Getting up a head of steam" made the steam powered automobile a slow starter getting out onto the road.

The gasoline engine is an internal combustion engine. Some people in early times thought of it as the explosion engine because it operates by a series of controlled explosions working a basic system of pistons, rods, and shafts geared into the rear wheels. The explosion engine was noisy and more complicated in adjustment and accessories. But it started with a flash and quickly got going.

Folks who had grown up in the horse age were wary about either type of automobile. With horses, it was a matter of understanding their personalities. A machine could not be talked to or persuaded. It

was remote. It made a person uneasy to sit near an engine in which explosions were going on all the time; but it was also well known that a superheated steam boiler exploded with a mighty big BANG!

The Stanley twins chose steam as their power source. The gasoline engine was new, still in its trial and error stage. They went with steam because its performance was proven and reliable in ships, trains and factories. It promised them plenty of power, too. It was the right choice at that time. For the next dozen years F.E. and F.O. designed and produced the superior-powered American automobile.

3.
The Coming of the
Stanley Steamer

The original Stanley Steamer, a neat little two-seater on spoked bicyclelike wheels, was ready in the autumn of 1897. The boiler and two cylinder steam engine were in a box on which the driver sat. The cylinders with the driving pistons inside were laid horizontally, in position to act "directly on the driving sprocket without intervening machinery of any kind." A chain belt stretching to a rear axle sprocket turned the wheels. It was like a bicycle gear arrangement with the twin pistons doing the work of human feet and muscle power.

It ran right along, but the twins were not satisfied. They built several more models, all as a hobby. They invented their own compact boiler, lightened the weight of the machinery. In the fall of 1898, they entered their steamer in an early New England automobile competition.

The hill-climb event allowed a standing start of only ten feet before the hill, which became steeper by degrees of five, ten, fifteen and twenty percent. No one believed any auto would even reach the twenty degree slope, but F.E. stepped up with a bit of advice:

"You'd better add on a stretch at thirty percent" he said. "I don't know if I can hold my steamer back!"

They did. The officials had just watched F.E. set a world record for '98 on their small dirt track—a mile in 2:11 (about thirty miles per hour). In the hill-climb, another steam car, a Whitney, led the gasoline and electric cars, climbing up so as to put its front wheels on the beginning of the twenty percent slope, but went no further. Then F.E. "shot" the Stanley Steamer to the top of the thirty percent incline with ease.

These successes attracted attention, and the inventors began to get many letters from people who wanted to buy Stanley Steamers. At about this time

George Eastman, the founder of the Kodak Company, offered them a fine price for their photographic patents and business, which the twins accepted.

One day F.O. and his wife set out upon a New England country drive—all the way to the top of Mount Washington, the highest peak in the East. More attention in the newspapers! The trailblazing automotive event was headlined as far away as Paris, France. F.E. and F.O. had not planned to become automobile manufacturers, but suddenly they had two hundred firm orders in hand, and their vacant Newton factory available as an assembly plant. So the twins agreed to cautiously expand their hobby, but vowed to remain as individual and inventive as always.

The Stanleys had barely begun manufacture of automobiles when a well-dressed gentleman walked into their Newton factory office.

"I am John Brisbane Walker, the owner of Cosmopolitan Magazine," he announced importantly, "and I have come to buy a half interest in your automobile business."

The twins looked at each other, and F.O. said: "I'm not sure we have a profitable business now, and we don't want a partner. We are quite satisfied working along together."

John Brisbane Walker went away disappointed. He was not used to being told no. A month later he was back to buy the Stanley Company. Just name your figure, he said. Well, the brothers did not want to sell so they asked what they thought was an impossible price—two hundred and fifty thousand dollars for a business just getting started.

"Exactly the figure I had in mind, a quarter million," agreed the rich publisher as he wrote out a deposit check. But though the Stanleys sold their patents, they remained in the auto business as experts at the new firm, the Locomobile Co. When the

Locomobile owners disagreed among themselves on company policy, it is said that for a short time each side had one Stanley twin as adviser.

F.E. and F.O. now decided to reenter the auto industry on their own. To compete with Locomobile and others they invented a new and better model of the Stanley Steamer. A principal improvement was the elimination of the chain drive arrangement. The compact boiler and engine were moved down under and geared directly to the rear axle.

The new car was a success and forced many other steam auto makers out of business at the beginning of the twentieth century—including Locomobile, who switched to building gasoline automobiles. Mr. Walker sold back the patents for which he had paid two hundred and fifty thousand dollars for just twenty-five thousand dollars, a fine profit for the Stanley twins.

4.

F.E. and F.O. Close Up

What were these clever brothers like close up? By habit and personality they remained Down East Maine country boys. Early morning found them sitting patiently on the front steps of the plant whittling as they awaited the arrival of their employee "family." Many were friends and neighbors from home, loyal and long-serving. It was said, Once a Stanley man, always a Stanley man.

Being mechanical geniuses, both F.E. and F.O. would become angered at the mistakes ordinary workers made and fire people. But the fired employee needed only to wait till F.E. or F.O. cooled down, or speak to the other twin, to be rehired. After the Stanley Steamer became really popular, about 1903, there were one hundred and forty employees. By 1918, the number had slowly grown to three hundred and fifty, a small force of skilled craftsmen building a world famous automobile.

F.E. and F.O. remained identical twins in every way, look-alikes to the curlings of their full beards, their bowler hats and their tight suits with stovepipe trousers. They were doubles on the job, too, taking turns at minding the office up front and the shop out back. Which brother had an employee spoken to? Few could tell. Fred Marriott, their shop foreman and racing driver, has said:

> They loved a good story. Didn't mind cuss words, but it had to be clean—and funny. Find one and tell it to him, and if it was F.E. he would bend over and slap his leg and say "Godfrey mighty!" and if it was F.O. he would bend over and slap his leg and say "Gee cracky!"

The customer who wanted to buy a Stanley Steamer wrote a very sincere letter asking to be allowed to own one. A Stanley automobile was something special and the twins wanted buyers to know and remember it. In due time, F.E. and F.O. would reply telling when to come and fetch it. A 1903 model sold for seven hundred and fifty dollars, a dollar a pound as it happened, in cash. You understand that buying anything on time payments was scarcely thought of in those days.

No guarantees were necessary, for if anyone complained about anything they were expected to return the Steamer and get their money back. The Stanley twins' pride in their product was very great! A demonstration ride with F.E. or F.O. was included in the price. Because the Stanley craftsmanship always remained wide open for possible improvements, it is said that no two Stanley Steamers were assembled exactly alike.

5.
An Extraordinary Automobile.

The performance of the Stanley was better than that of the gasoline auto of that day. It was able to use over ninety percent of the power its steam generated. Gasoline engines of that time only used about thirty-five percent of their fuel energy.

Most automobiles in the 1980s have "automatic transmissions" to change the gears handling the flow of power from the piston to the wheels, but you can feel and hear the gears changing as they help the gasoline engine keep the car moving. In the early days gear shifting was done by hand and managing the clutch pedal with one foot was difficult. Jerking, stalling, clanging of gears were common. "Grind me up a pound!" was a wisecrack shouted at the awkward driver.

Driving a Stanley in 1903 was as smooth as driving a modern car with automatic transmission. Remember the improvement the Stanley twins made in their second generation of Steamers—steam pressure, generated by heating a compact boiler by a kerosene-fed firing burner, was applied to twin pistons geared directly into the rear wheels. It is claimed that a Stanley had only thirteen interior moving parts, a simple construction that saved on wear. A pedal on the floor ran the car forward or backward; a lever on the steering column set the desired speed.

You couldn't stall a Stanley Steamer. The steady, ever-present steam pressure was the reason. If run up against a solid wall the steamer might grind off its rear wheels without giving up! One other feature of steam pressure built up in the boiler was that a reserve could be held back, and a Steamer could run on a mile or two after its fire was out. Also, a head of steam allowed a quick getaway. An oldtime Stanley accelerated from zero to sixty miles per hour in eleven seconds. Neat! And the smoothness of its departure has been compared with that of a yacht

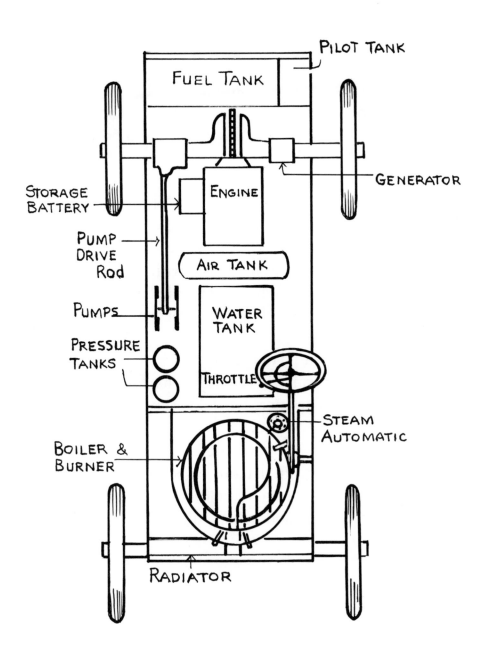

PILOT TANK

FUEL TANK

GENERATOR

STORAGE
BATTERY

ENGINE

PUMP
DRIVE
ROD

AIR TANK

PUMPS

WATER
TANK

PRESSURE
TANKS

THROTTLE

STEAM
AUTOMATIC

BOILER &
BURNER

RADIATOR

leaving its mooring . . . and as quietly too, for the later models, which recycled most of their steam, were nearly silent. An ultrasonic hiss did bring dogs a-running though!

The early models, breathing out clouds of steam, gave off a muffled, watery "Shooga-Shooga" panting sound. They only got a mile to a gallon of water. Luckily there were then plenty of horse drinking troughs to be found. A hose with a hand pump was fitted to the car. The driver pulled up to a handy trough, got out, flipped in the nozzle and pumped up a supply of water.

The story is told of a horse that was pushed aside as the mechanical marvel drank its fill—and left hardly a drop. The angry nag laid back its ears, bared teeth and bit the Stanley!

A Vermont legislator tried to make a law that these "snorting steam demons be barred by law from facilities set out for the comfort and well-being of man's noble friend and helper, the horse."

6.
Oh, The Stories They Told!

Because they dared to be different and did it so well, the Stanley twins' products probably inspired more tales than any other brand of automobile. Here are some of these legends of the road—you may decide for yourself which are true, and most of them *could* have been.

Main rail crossings used to be watched by a crossing guard, who either swung a bar across the road, or waved a flag when a train approached. It is told that some Stanley Steamers had train engine whistles. As they slipped quietly across the tracks they would toot—and out would come the watchman to raise the barrier and wait for the train that didn't come.

The early Stanley automobiles looked much like an ordinary horse buggy (that's why "horseless carriage"). One day the twins quietly came up to a rail crossing where the guard was napping. F.O. awoke him with the question:

"Have you seen our horse anywhere?"

"No, sir; I have not." replied the man as he dazedly peered at the double image of the brothers seated in their carriage, "but if I can help, I'll be glad to do so."

"Never mind," said F.E., "I think I see him in that patch of woods ahead."

"Well then, let's get on up there!" declared F.O. easing the Steamer into silent forward motion while the poor watchman looked on bug-eyed with amazement.

F.E. knew how to work this trick even better. A stop for lunch in some little town allowed the Steamer to cool off. So a new head of steam pressure needed to be heated up before the auto could start up again. F.E. turned up the burner beneath the boiler, made very fine adjustments, and left the throttle open just a bit. He'd walk out ahead of the Steamer, maybe a hundred feet, and talk with the local folks until exactly the right moment. Then, pulling out his watch, F.E. would announce:

"Godfrey mighty! Almost two o'clock. I must be on my way." Turning toward the Steamer he'd whistle and call out: "Giddap, Napoleon!"

And the auto, having just then built up enough steam pressure in its boiler to move the pistons, rolled obediently forward to match F.E.'s fine sense of timing.

Those gasoline or kerosene-fed burners beneath the boiler could flicker until flooded—then suddenly lick out to one side a three-foot tongue of flame that would scatter pedestrians. The Stanley Manual counseled the driver not to worry and to continue slowly till the extra fuel burned off. We are told that more than one flaming Stanley was doused with water by horse-drawn fire wagons pulling alongside.

People were concerned about what a Stanley Steamer could, or would do. Might the boiler blow up? No. The Stanley twins designed their boiler tubing to leak under extreme pressure, not to explode. But the suspicion lingered . . .

F.O. traveled by train to New Orleans with a Steamer. There was no interstate highway system then, very few paved roads anywhere in America. It was the first Stanley the city had seen. When it was assembled, F.O. lit the burner and twisted knobs and valves. Satisfied, he climbed aboard. BANG!! The crowd ran away.

"Gee cracky! that was a loud one." murmured F.O. He was not excited. He checked the boiler, the fuel tank, and all four tires. Nothing had exploded. Then he looked at what was left of his audience— just two kids laughing so hard they looked as if they might burst. Underneath the car were paper shreds from a big firecracker! F.O. didn't get upset. Here was a good publicity stunt. He decided to get a supply of firecrackers for himself.

Stanley Steamers could be set into reverse gear while in forward motion and sometimes this ability was used for braking. Since they could travel equally fast forward or backward, there are tales of daredevils overtaking and passing other traffic—accelerating backwards!

And, finally, Stanley man Fred Marriott tells a story of a time in an early Massachusetts road race when he was coming up to the finish line at over sixty miles per hour. The curious crowd pushed danger-ously into the road ahead. Marriott reversed. Amid a shrieking of jammed rubber and wrenching vibra-tions the front part of the racer, which momentum dragged forward, tore free from the rear-geared (and rear-minded) backend!

7.
The Wogglebug of 1906-07

The twins loved speed and competed with each other in setting time records between their Massachusetts factory and the old home place in Maine. They made an excellent record in general auto racing, especially in hill climb events. The gasoline automobilers disliked this superiority. They muttered about "freaks" spoiling their competitions. Naturally, the Stanley reaction was:

"Gee cracky; we'll really show them!"

In 1906, they created the Wogglebug (named after "Thoroughly Educated (T.E.) Wogglebug" a man-sized know-it-all talking insect from the Land of Oz). It would be a world-beater, the best racer of its times.

The Wogglebug looked somewhat like a canoe

set upside down upon high, bicyclelike wheels. It was the first auto racer designed from a study of air flow, with what we call streamlining. The body was smooth and rounded and the driver enclosed "in-line" so as not to bulge into the air stream. The twins had whittled out wooden models and performed air-flow tests on them, pioneering what airplane builders do today in the wind tunnels of their design labs.

To drive this streamlined racer into the record books, its boiler accumulated about one thousand pounds pressure, at least twice that of the standard Stanley. And all that mass of tiny copper tubing inside the boiler was there to provide the maximum heating surface for the conversion of water into steam pressure and keep it that way. The one hundred and fifty horsepower that pressure made available to do the work of driving the wheels is less than half that of modern automobiles, but in the Woggle-bug it didn't have to push so much bulk.

The body was plywood to lessen the overall weight. What weight there was was mainly in the rear end of the Wogglebug, because the engine and boiler were close to the rear axle, which turned the wheels. This would cause a disaster in the future. But not this year . . .

ENGINE: Rear-sited; 2 cylinders; 4½″ bore; 6½″ stroke; Cubic capacity—206″; Maximum power —to 150 hp.

BOILER: 30″ diameter by 18″ depth; 1,475 ½″ copper tubes with heating surface of 285 sq. ft.; Steam pressure—800 to 900 lb. per sq. in. CHASSIS: Plywood body; Steering tiller stick; an in-line cockpit; 34″ wire-spoke wheels with 3″ motorcycle tires pressured to 60 lbs. per sq. in. WEIGHT: 2,195 lbs.

Fred Marriot in the
Wogglebug

Stanley Racing Car of 1906

The Wogglebug was the Stanley's featured entry at the 1906 winter races on the hard-packed seaside sands at Ormond Beach, Florida (just north of to-day's racers' haven at Daytona Beach), and it really did *show them*. The sleek racer badly beat its gaso-line-fueled competition as it sped at 127.66 miles per hour! Fred Marriott thereby became the first person on our planet to move faster than two miles per minute—and that's no tall tale. It's in the record books. Man in the air in 1906 had barely flown faster than thirty miles per hour. (The airplane hadn't been invented till 1903.)

Not much was heard from the gasoline crowd about "Wait till next year!" Instead they talked about barring steam automobiles from the races. That would be a sure way to "beat" them. But no official action was taken. Meanwhile the Stanley twins readied their plans to really sock it to them the next year.

The Wogglebug of 1907 looked almost the same as the record-setting model, but underneath the wood shell throbbed a good deal more power. Its boiler was designed to contain thirteen hundred pounds pressure!

Matters got off to a contrary start in Florida. The Wogglebug had been damaged in shipment south. Of course it had arrived by rail—to drive from Boston to Florida in 1907 was an adventure that would take a week or two. Then, the beach was in only fair condition for the speed of the Wogglebug. Recent stormy weather had soaked the sand and also wave-warped the flat surface here and there.

Then the gas boys tried to put one over on the Stanley men. They knew that F.E. always went to bed very early. So later that evening, while he slept, they changed the time of the morning's first trial run from 9 A.M. to 7 A.M. But they forgot that F.E. went to bed early because, from his youth on the farm, he always got up with the chickens—at 4:30 A.M. So he learned of the change and pulled a sleepy Fred Marriott out of bed and got him into the racer in time to win.

∞ 8. ∞
Taking OFF!

On the evening before the final, most important time trial, F.E. and his driver toured the beach and made special note of a likely trouble spot. Two small sand ridges ran down across the beach raceway and between them was a shallow dip in the surface. Fingering his flowing black moustachios confidently, Fred Marriott told F.E.:

"The next time I'll hit those ripples so fast I'll skim right over them."

The morning of January 27, 1907, dawned cool and gray after rain. The Wogglebug, with a boiler triple-wrapped with piano wire to contain its immense reserve of steam pressure, cruised up the beach for a head start on its famous time trial. Then the steam wizard of speed turned about and began its legendary run for glory.

"Here it comes!" yelled the crowd as the cherry red Wogglebug, trailing a mighty plume of steam, rushed down upon them.

"There it goes!" they screamed as the racer whipped by them in a scarlet blur. The electric timer started, and F.E. snapped his stop watch.

Faster and faster rushed the racer along the beach as the Wogglebug delivered its ready reserve of steam pressure to the pounding pistons. Fred Marriott believed a new speed record was in the making. He heard it in the whistle of wind, felt it in the frantic tempo of the machine. Then they hit the ripples in the sand.

Bounce! over the first sand swell; WHOMP! into the dip. Then, in clearing the second hump, the Wogglebug's lighter front end poked up and hung lifted there by the rush of air currents pushing beneath its flat undercarriage. Disaster was in the making as the airborne front end began to turn seaward. Marriott waggled the steering tiller attached to the front wheels, of course—uselessly. Then the skidding drag of the earthbound rear wheels took hold and the racer's nose dropped toward the beach —but somewhat *sideways!*

C-RRR-A-SHH!! It ripped, it tore, and rolled and shattered. Unstoppable momentum pushed and crushed the splintering plywood chassis until it separated. The front portion, with Marriott wrapped within, rolled and skidded on down the sands, while the freed engine and boiler bounded into the surf to hiss and roar beneath mounting columns of steam.

"Godfrey mighty!"

A distressed F.E. Stanley then and there swore a binding oath never to race again. Employees were like family to the Stanleys. It was too dangerous!

It hardly seemed possible that Fred Marriott lay alive and semiconscious in the forward wreckage. Though cut, scraped and bruised in many places he had escaped dangerous internal injuries. Good luck saw him through to a complete recovery.

Of course no record was recorded. F.E. closed his stop watch the instant he saw the Wogglebug waver, and afterwards measuring to that point decided that its speed was then above one hundred and thirty miles per hour—with the possibility of one hundred and fifty miles per hour that day in 1907. He also found that the front wheels had been lifted off the ground for a remarkable span of one hundred and three feet!

❧ 9. ❧
Falling Back

F.E. kept his word. Therefore we do not know how fast a yearly improved Stanley steam racer would have moved. This uncertainty inspired that famous, false story about the one thousand dollar three-minute throttle reward. And the end of racing matched a beginning decline of Stanley Steamers. You see, races were important proving grounds of technical excellence then, just as today, and they brought to the Stanley Company publicity it really needed.

This was because F.E. and F.O. didn't believe in advertising their product. Their pride in their automobile made such a public appeal seem gross. From

the beginning, their proposition was: Between ourselves we are building the finest automobile possible
for ourselves. If you want one, too, ask us about it.
The twins did not care at all about putting a Stanley
Steamer into every American garage. They went
along doing their own thing and paid little attention
to what was going on in Detroit, which had become
the center for gasoline-engine car-making.

They should have given it more notice!

Getting any early automobile started was a nasty
job. It took the average motorist about a half hour
to perform the "Stanley Drill" in bringing the boiler
to the right steam pressure: Light and adjust the
burner, twist valves, open and shut knobs, read
gauges. Folks thought you had to be half an engineer
to operate one.

Gasoline autos were awkward too—they were
cranked by hand; and if a backfire occurred, look
out! The crank kicked back hard and could break the
arm of a human starter. Then, in 1912, electric *self-
starters* appeared on gasoline autos. The steam automobile industry never developed easier starting.

For some years before this F.E. and F.O. were
no longer closely working together, and their sepa-
ration surely had something to do with the decline
of the Stanley Steamer. F.O. had become ill with

the very dangerous lung disease called tuberculosis. Antibiotics were unknown, but high, dry air was thought to be of aid. Tuberculosis patients in the early years of the twentieth century went out west, often to the high plains and mountain slopes of Colorado. F.O. settled at Colorado Springs.

There, far from the area of auto industry, he went into the hotel business, and the Stanley Hotel, an elegant resort, was the result. In connection with this project he saw the need for a special kind of limousine to carry tourists about in the Colorado mountains, and the Stanley Company provided a steam mountain model, the first "station wagon" type automobile. He also made use of the artistic bent he shared with F.E. and became a successful manufacturer of violins.

F.E., meanwhile, was working on the problem of building a steam driven "unit car" to replace the streetcars of those times. He was en route in his Stanley Steamer to a conference on this subject when on a Massachusetts country road he was abruptly faced with a roadblock caused by two farm wagons stopped together while their drivers chatted. To avoid hitting them F.E. drove off the road, crashed, and was killed. The year was 1918, and a saddened F.O. had not the heart or will to head the automobile company. It passed to outsiders and, in 1925, closed. F.O. lived on to be ninety-one years old.

Modern Memories

A good place to see a Stanley Steamer today is at an antique auto meet. The owner of a Stanley is likely to think the idea of the steam automobile is not old-fashioned, but very modern; that a modern Steamer could be built that would be simply started and ready to go in half a minute or less. It would be quietly powerful and efficient, use any cheap, plentiful fuel to stoke its boiler, and not foul the air noticeably with its exhaust vapors. People who own Stanley Steamers, then and now, are proud and loyal.

Just one more story!

Back in the 1950s, there was an auto garage in Newton, Massachusetts, just a few blocks from the old Stanley plant. The garageman was a plain-spoken, hearty old fellow then seventy-five years old. He was Fred Marriott, the one hundred and fifty(?) miles per hour driver who had dared fate and lived long. What was his specialty? Why, the repair of Stanley Steamers, exclusively!

F.E. and F.O. would have understood. Once a Stanley man, always a Stanley man.

❦ Bibliography ❦

BOOKS

Bentley, John: *Oldtime Steam Cars* (1953)   The encyclopedic book on all steam automobiles. Twenty illustrated pages on Stanley Steamers.

Clifton, Paul: *The Fastest Men on Earth* (1966)   A chapter about the record setting Wogglebug.

Derr, Thomas: *The Modern Steam Car and Its Background* (1932)   Authorized by a last-gasp steam car manufacturer, it has good Stanley history and lore.

Ellis, Stanley W.: *Smogless Days* (1971) About contemporary Stanley fanciers, with excellent modern photographs.

Jackson, Robert B.: *The Steam Cars of the Stanley Twins* (1969) Sober, thorough tech-oriented book for children with photo illustrations.

Weiss, Harvey: *Motors & Engines & How They Work* (1969) Excellent juvenile on the subject.

Woodbury, George: *Story of a Stanley Steamer* (1950) A modern owner's love affair illumined by excellent historical anecdote.

PERIODICALS

American Heritage: "The Stanleys & Their Steamer" by John Carlova Popular treatment, photos and line drawings. February 1959.

Automobile Quarterly: "Stanley Steamer Fact & Fancy" A demythification of the automobile drawn from statements by Raymond Stanley, son of F.E. Summer 1963.

Cycle & Automobile Trade Journal: "The Stanley Steam Wagons" A technical article with photos of current Stanley models and gear illustrations. May 1903.

Harpers: "The Steaming Stanley Twins" Howard D. Fabing Popular treatment, a few line drawings. October 1959.